This colourful book covers numbers 1 to 10.
Each number is boldly illustrated with
pictures of familiar objects arranged in their
correct numerical pattern.
Further practice is given in matching, sorting
and counting through a variety of lively colour
pictures, making this book both enjoyable and
invaluable for any young child.

*Available in Series S808*

\* **a is for apple**
\* **I can count**
**Tell me the time**
**Colours and shapes**
\* **Nursery Rhymes**

**\****Also available as* Ladybird Teaching Friezes

Published by Ladybird Books Ltd  Loughborough  Leicestershire  UK
Ladybird Books Inc  Lewiston  Maine 04240  USA
© LADYBIRD BOOKS LTD MCMLXXX

# I can count

illustrated by LYNN N GRUNDY

Ladybird Books

one

frog

# 2
## two

2 soldiers

3

three

teddy bears

four

**mugs**

# 5

## five

5 eggs

**six**

snails

seven

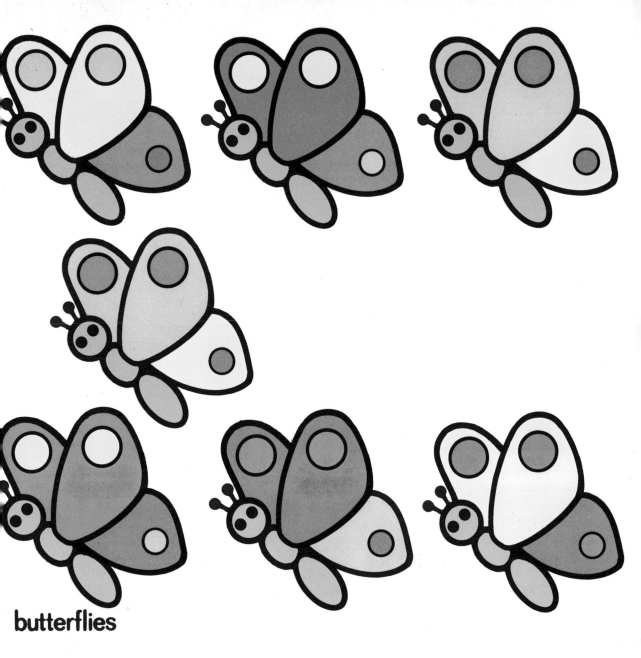

**butterflies**

eight

8 balls

nine

apples

10 buttons

How many people are sitting in the bus?
How many people are waiting for a ride?
How many people are there altogether?

# What does the witch need for her spell?
## How many . . . .

bats?

toadstools?

spiders?

frogs?

snails?

lizards?

# Can each monkey have one banana?

Which cars will be numbers 2, 5 and 9?
Who is driving car number 7?

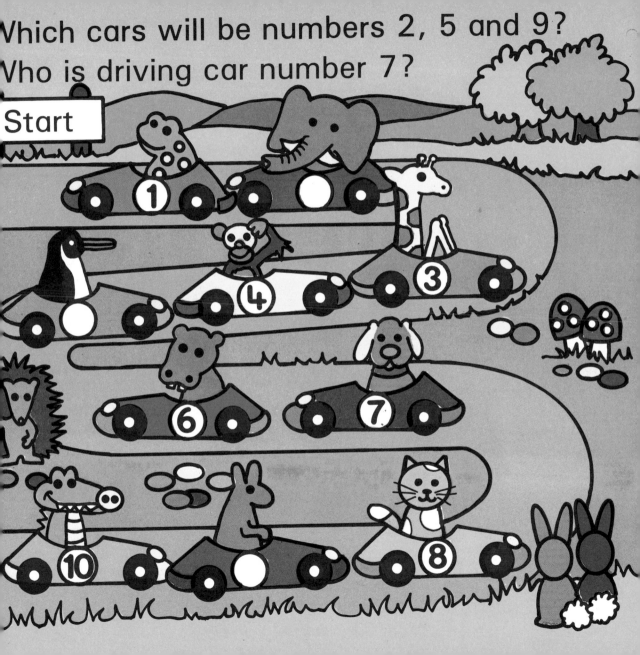

# Count the different things in the picture